The *Joy* of Your Salvation

REFLECTIONS ON
THE PSALMS
OF LENT

Deborah McCann

TWENTY-THIRD PUBLICATIONS
A Division of Bayard   MYSTIC, CT 06355

—

Twenty-Third Publications
A Division of Bayard
185 Willow Street
P.O. Box 180
Mystic, CT 06355
(860) 536-2611
(800) 321-0411
www.twentythirdpublications.com

ISBN:1-58595-181-1
Library of Congress Catalog Card Number: 2001135965
Printed in the U.S.A.

Dedication

*To Dan and Michael,
who share and inspire my faith journey.
Thank you for the joy you bring
to each and every day.*

The Joy
of Your
Salvation

Introduction

It has always struck me as odd—this season of deep penitence and introspection right as the earth begins to burgeon with new life. But Lent is, in fact, a season of profound, abiding joy, a time for celebrating God's overwhelming mercy and love for us. As springtime begins to make itself felt, we too feel anxious and eager for renewal and change.

Nowhere in the Scriptures will you find voices that echo these human longings more than in the psalms. There you meet believers who rail at God, who mourn loudly and scream about life's unfairness, who praise God's justice and mercy, who seek God's help in times of fear and doubt and loss. You will often find anger and praise mixed in the same psalm. These are very human voices, ones that speak from the heart with the most basic and elemental emotions, voices that seek God in joy, in sorrow, in pain, in anger, and in trust.

You'll find many lenten commentaries that ask you to focus on the gospels of the season. Here, I would ask you to look at the poetry and raw emotion of the psalms. Through these songs of yearning, loss, repentance, and triumph, you may hear your own voice, and can join in praising the wonder and glory of a God who restores to us the joy of God's salvation (Psalm 51).

So, for Ash Wednesday and every day of Lent thereafter, I invite you to read the psalm of the day. It doesn't take a long time, and a phrase or two may stay with you all day long. Pray over the psalm and listen to what the Lord is telling you. I offer the reflections, questions, and prayers here as a starting-off point for your own spiritual journey.

May your lenten journey be fruitful, positive, and filled with joy, so that at Easter, your "Alleluia!" will ring from the rafters in praise and thanksgiving for the wonders our God has done and continues to do.

Ash Wednesday

Psalm 51

Sustain in me a willing spirit...

Exploring the verses

O Lord, open my lips, and my mouth will declare your praise.

As I leave church marked with my ashes, will I immediately get back to "business as usual," or will I be truly marked as a disciple, today and always?

Create in me a clean heart, O God, and put a new and right spirit within me.

Will my witness of faith shout joyfully of good news, or will I stand sternly in judgment on those whose reasons for not coming to church regularly I can never begin to imagine?

Reflection

Churches are full on Ash Wednesday. People you never see on a weekly basis file humbly down the aisle to receive on their foreheads the symbol of our mortality and our dependence on the mercy of God.

Sometimes these people are chided and scolded for only showing up a couple of times a year. Remonstrance has its place, I'm sure, yet when I look at the faces of the people moving toward the priest to receive their ashes, I see great hope. For at least at this moment on this day we all have a desire to change our hearts, to have a willing spirit, to make Lent a time of renewal. "Repent and believe the Good News." The gracious, unfathomable love of God for us is good news—we should be welcoming and celebrating the presence of our occasional visitors. Maybe this is the day—the acceptable time—when all our lives will change, and our hearts will be opened.

Turning to God

Lord, sustain in me a willing spirit. I want to do your will and spread the good news of your love and mercy to all. Let your light shine through me on all I meet, and let "Welcome!" be the first word I utter to everyone.

Thought in Action

Let us seek to make this Lent a time of welcome and comfort for those we meet.

Thursday after Ash Wednesday

Psalm 1

The Lord watches over the way of the righteous.

Exploring the verses

Happy are those who do not follow the advice of the wicked...

Am I too quick to give in to the temptations of the quick fix, choosing "fast" over "good" just to line my own coffers?

...or sit in the seat of scoffers.

Worse, do I work halfheartedly, nursing contempt for those in authority, that they won't notice the difference?

Reflection

It's the day after Ash Wednesday, and already I read this psalm with a note of skepticism. "Happy are those...[whose] delight is in the law of the Lord.... In all that they do, they prosper." That doesn't sound like a lot of people I know whose lives are dedicated firmly to the Lord's service. It doesn't reflect the experience of many people in Third World countries whose eyes are fixed on the Lord and the gospel, but who suffer from inhuman poverty and vicious repression.

So what gives? In this world, it would seem, the way of the wicked hardly vanishes, it flourishes. Society today champions those who succeed no matter what it takes; one-upsmanship is applauded; cold-blooded "it's only business" attitudes are considered praiseworthy.

But there is another path. And it requires faith. It falls to those who trust the Lord and walk the Lord's paths to begin to make a difference, to give voice to the voiceless, to proclaim our conviction that the Good News *is* good news. We can do this with confidence and impunity—if we truly believe what we claim to believe. A little more healthy trust and a little less worldly skepticism might make all the difference.

Turning to God

Lord, guide my footsteps. Give me the strength and courage to witness your good news to all I meet. Let me trust in your promise, and proclaim it ever and always.

Thought in Action

Today, let's try to make a difference—for the better—in someone's life.

Friday after
Ash Wednesday

Psalm 51

You have no delight in sacrifice.

Exploring the verses

I know my transgressions, and my sin is ever before me.

How much of a given day do I spend cheerfully accomplishing what needs to be done, and how much time do I spend calling attention to my mighty deeds?

The sacrifice acceptable to God is a broken spirit; a broken and contrite heart, O God, you will not despise.

When I see the example of others' witness, am I inspired—or envious? Humility is such a hard thing to learn!

Reflection

Here's another sign of contradiction. God is not pleased with sacrifices. So that means when I agree to do something for a friend on a regular basis, and that friend's expectations suddenly increase, and I go along with the changes with a smile on my face and my heart black with rage and self-pity at how I'm being put upon and taken advantage of YET AGAIN, that kind of sacrifice won't be pleasing to God?

Imagine that! God's not interested in the outward show of how much we do for people, or how loudly we proclaim our virtue or complain at how little time we have for ourselves because we're always on the go, doing for others. God's interested in the state of our hearts, the *why* behind our actions. God asks us not so much to *do*, but to *be*. God wants us to be humble and childlike, open and trusting, compassionate and giving because these qualities mirror God's own. If God were to take umbrage at our demands, none of us would survive! And yet we do, because God is God, and—may God's name be praised—God's ways are not ours!

Turning to God

Lord, your heart is pure and true and fueled by love. Help me see goodness and light where I can only see darkness and hate. For your light shines everywhere, if we only have eyes to see it.

Thought in Action

Today, let's let God work through us, and stay out of God's way!

Saturday after Ash Wednesday

Psalm 86

Save your servant who trusts in you.

Exploring the verses

Be gracious to me, O Lord, for to you do I cry all day long.

Do I bargain and wheedle with God? Do I challenge and whine when I don't get my way?

Gladden the soul of your servant.

Do I pray for results, not strength and courage—for things, not qualities?

Reflection

This psalm is full of pleading, almost wheedling at times: "Answer me, for I am poor and needy...Be gracious to me, for to you I cry all day long...Listen to my cry of supplication." This sounds like a lot of my prayers—the bargaining, the self-deprecation, the whining.

But here's the beauty part, even acknowledged by the psalmist: "For you, O Lord, are good and forgiving, *abounding in steadfast love to all who call on you.*" God's kindness and mercy shine everywhere and always, even when we, in our blindness to anyone's needs but our own, can't see them. Our blindness can be much deeper than that—sometimes we can't even see God's bounty surrounding us with its beauty and grace. I think of a time when my husband came excitedly home from work and bundled us into the car to drive and look at the extraordinary fall foliage. I missed it all; I was busy complaining about deadlines. How much I needed to learn!

God's kindness and mercy are for *all* who call on God—even those people we might not think deserving of such bounty, even those whose pleas are at cross-purposes with our own. Do we have enough faith to trust in God's wisdom?

Turning to God

Dear Lord, help me be a servant who trusts in you. Help me see the needs of others as well as my own, and celebrate with real joy when it seems that their prayers have been answered and mine haven't. Help me to know that your grace surrounds me even when I can't feel it.

Thought in Action

Today, let's thank God for all God's goodness.

First Sunday
of Lent (A)

Psalm 51

My sin is ever before me.

Exploring the verses

Do not take your holy spirit from me.

Do I believe that God is with me even in the darkest times?

According to your abundant mercy blot out my transgressions.

Have I gotten out of my own way long enough to feel God's gentle presence in my life?

Reflection

How naked in longing, sincere in contrition, and vibrant with hope this psalm is! The psalmist possesses something a lot of us, I'm sure, wish we had—a sure and steady faith and trust in the Lord's goodness and compassion.

The psalmist is on familiar terms with God—abject in misery, but not despairing of God's ready ear and sure mercy. I know there are times in my prayer life when I've wished for such certainty and conviction.

Lent is a season of penitence, yes, but penitence is about conversion, turning our hearts to God. And the amazing thing is, when we do open ourselves up to the wonderful, all-encompassing love that God offers, it is there, ready and waiting to enfold us. Not that we'll always be aware of it, not that we'll have some sharp, startling moment of epiphany, not that we'll suddenly be suffused with joy. It's often more like the "still, small sound" that inspired Elijah—something we don't even recognize except in retrospect. Even more often, perhaps, it's nothing at all that we can name, or sense, or notice. But if we begin to see with new eyes, realizing that our sins may be ever before us but are already forgiven and forgotten by our merciful God, then perhaps this Lent will become a time of great thanksgiving and quiet rejoicing.

Turning to God

Dear Lord, if wishing made it so, I would proclaim your promises from the rooftops. Help me trust and rely on your goodness and mercy, every moment of my life.

Thought in Action

Try to find at least one moment today that speaks to you of God.

First Sunday
of Lent (B)

Psalm 25

He teaches the humble his way.

Exploring the verses

Lead me in your truth, and teach me.

Do I put my own opinions aside long enough to listen to God in my life?

Make me to know your ways, O Lord.

When I do try to listen to God's voice, can I hear it through all the static and interference of the world around me?

Reflection

I was at Mass one Sunday recently, ready as always to offer "constructive criticism" of the event. I've worked in religious publishing a long time, and it's taught me just enough about the church to make me the worst kind of loose cannon. I can nitpick with the best of them, and frequently do. Not the best grounding for being humble and teachable, I admit, and God often has a surprise in store.

This particular Sunday, the presider was chugging through the Eucharistic Prayer at a great clip ("Source and summit of our liturgical life," I thought, "yeah, right!"). Suddenly he stopped dead. He had completely forgotten his place, and was standing there, holding the chalice and paten elevated before him, with no clue about what came next. The momentary panic was evident in his eyes.

From the front pew came a small voice. "Through him, and with him, and in him...," said a man who is a client at our local mental health facility, one of those people often quickly dismissed at the sign of peace, and otherwise hurried by on the way out the door. Father came to himself, and completed the Doxology, and I knelt there grateful and humbled. Who was paying better attention to God's life and presence that day? Who was reaching out to help? Thank God for Sundays like these! One day I hope to be a part of the solution, not the problem.

Turning to God

Dear Lord, make me more teachable. Open my eyes and ears to your word and work ever and always in my life.

Thought into Action

Today, let's try to seek out someone who can teach us more about God.

13

First Sunday
of Lent (C)

Psalm 91

No evil shall befall you.

Exploring the verses

They will bear you up, so that you will not dash your foot against a stone.

Do I believe myself always under God's care? Or do I fear that God's mind often wanders where I'm concerned?

I will be with them in trouble.

When have I felt God's presence and comfort and known it?

Reflection

On one memorable morning, a friend of mine had a frozen pipe that burst, two children with chicken pox, a car that wouldn't start, and the rejection of a children's book manuscript. She called me in tears. "You know that stupid saying about how God never gives you more than you can handle? I think it's a bunch of junk!"

I couldn't agree with her more. That's why this psalm is alternately a source of great comfort and an example of incredible faith. We've all had days that called us to question just how much more we can take. We've all had rough times in our lives, our careers, our marriages, and our families that can seriously challenge us and even make us question our belief in a loving and merciful God.

There's a prayer I like in these times that seems to sum up the promise and solace offered in this psalm. I'm not sure of the original source, but it goes something like this: "Lord, help me to remember that nothing is going to happen to me today that you and I together can't handle." Even these words seem overly facile when we're faced with grave situations in our lives. However, they can help keep us focused on the idea that it's one step at a time that wins the race, one day at a time that treats the addiction, one moment at a time that either destroys or can rekindle a damaged relationship.

Turning to God

Dear Lord, moment by moment, second by second, renew my trust in you. Help me build a sure foundation that will open my heart to your will.

Thought into Action

Let's suspend disbelief today, and find something or someone we can trust completely.

Monday
of the First Week

Psalm 19

Let the words of my mouth and the meditation of my heart be acceptable to you.

Exploring the verses

The law of the Lord is perfect, reviving the soul...the precepts of the Lord are right, rejoicing the heart.

Are the promises of God just too good to be true? Do I have trouble even picturing them, much less believing them?

The decrees of the Lord are sure, making wise the simple.

Are there ways I can change my life, to act "as if" I believe, so that my faith might be strengthened?

Reflection

Sometimes you can get so down that it starts to look like up (my apologies for mangling a popular book title). At times like this, no amount of encouragement or pep talks will ever convince you that things can be better. Prayers are empty; faith is a joke. If you should find yourself in this position, and you're lucky enough to know someone in a 12-step program, ask that person how different life is now from when they started. If you're close to this person, and have walked through their recovery with them, chances are you've been able to see the light come back into their eyes, and to witness the blossoming of renewed hope. It has been my great gift to know many people who have truly come back to life through recovery. They live life more easily; they have come to know the simplicity and wonder of quiet joy—and this in the midst of everyday problems. And it all began with trust.

The benefits or promises of walking with the Lord and following God's ways are all on display in this psalm. At the wonder of the glory they promise each and every one of us, we can only beg that the words of our mouths might do them justice, and that we may be true and certain witnesses of the Good News of God.

Turning to God

Dear Lord, your promises of abundance can sometimes seem hollow in my day-to-day life. Help me to experience some of the joy of your salvation, so that my words—and my life—will do you justice.

Thought in Action

Today, let's try to look for signs of God's power and goodness in everyone—especially those people we find it hardest to deal with.

Tuesday
of the First Week

Psalm 34

The Lord is near to the brokenhearted.

Exploring the verses

I sought the Lord, and he answered me, and delivered me from all my fears.

Have I felt this confidence and joy in my life? How? When?

When the righteous cry for help, the Lord hears, and rescues them from all their troubles.

Do I really believe this? Can I still see God's presence even when I am in distress?

Reflection

This has to be one of the most comforting, reassuring, affirming psalms in the whole canon. Images of love and care abound: "Look to him, and be radiant; so your faces shall never be ashamed.... The eyes of the Lord are on the righteous, and his ears are open to their cry.... The Lord is near to the brokenhearted, and saves the crushed in spirit."

More often than not, I'm convinced that, beautiful as this psalm is, it has no bearing on our life and times. And then I meet someone whose example of God's goodness and bounty just spills out and showers everyone with a warmth and a love that is palpable. Nothing seems impossible for people like this—their faith is joyous, their joy rests firmly on trust, and their trust is immovable.

These are the people who remind me that it's the words of comfort, the strong shoulders to bear us up, and the warm arms to hold us tight as we weep (as well as wrap us in bear hugs of unrestrained joy) that reflect God's presence. God needs us to do God's work in this fractured, frenzied world of ours. We are the ones who are to work for justice, practice mercy, and do all humbly.

Our God is a God of light and love, a God who wants to wipe away our tears and hold us close. Let us go and do likewise.

Turning to God

Dear Lord, help me bring justice and mercy to our world. Let others see your radiance shining through me. Give me the courage and conviction to be good news to everyone I meet.

Thought in Action

Today, let's do everything we can to make others "radiant with joy."

Wednesday
of the First Week

Psalm 51

Your abundant mercy.

Exploring the verses

Put a new and right spirit within me.

How have I felt God's compassion in my own life? Do I try to be compassionate with others?

If I were to give a burnt offering, you would not be pleased.

Are my motives of service as pure as they can be? Am I truly working to build the kingdom, or to feather my own nest?

Reflection

The only way we can really see God's compassion at work is in the lives of those around us. For example, let me tell you about two people I know. There's a woman in my city who runs a small convenience store. She's smart, she's savvy, and she's tough. People don't mess with her. There's a gentleman in my city who is a client at the local mental health outreach center. A gentler, more childlike soul you'd be hard pressed to meet. Once, when this gentleman was going to take a short train journey, the store owner made sure he had a telephone to call her, a number where she could be reached at all times, and some extra money to make sure he'd be able to get home. This is a side of her not everybody sees. But her witness is clear and strong, and because of her compassion, other people in the city look out for our friend, too. So the circle widens....

Compassion, unending and unqualified, is what God offers us. We have a choice each day to build the kingdom or break it down. Knowing how much God loves us, though, how can we not go out into the fields and marketplaces, spreading the good news of new life and new hope? And all it takes to begin are eyes open enough to see, and arms wide enough to embrace.

Turning to God

Dear Lord, your goodness and compassion fill me with awe, and unworthiness to accept your gracious gift. Yet I will accept it, and use it as best I can, to bring the good news of your light and life to everyone I meet.

Thought in Action

Today, let our words and deeds help even one person know God's mercy and love.

Thursday
of the First Week

Psalm 138

Do not forsake the work of your hands.

Exploring the verses

On the day I called, you answered me, you increased my strength of soul.

If I have been blessed to feel the Lord's strength, how can I witness this strength for others?

Your steadfast love, O Lord, endures forever.

In those times when I (or others) find these words hard to believe, what can I do to renew my trust in God?

Reflection

In the city where I live, some of the residents are engaged in a battle of David and Goliath proportions. An international conglomerate has already started building its global headquarters here. In the hope of revitalizing the city and attracting more businesses and tourism, the local development board has been buying up properties to make room for a hotel, health center, and upscale condominiums. The problem is that some of the property owners didn't want to sell—they had an established, comfortable neighborhood, and felt they were being displaced.

As the words flowing back and forth have grown more biting and less civil, the conviction of the people who want to stay has taken on a twist unusual enough to attract front-page attention in the local newspaper—some of them have turned to prayer. Each Thursday morning a group gathers and walks through the streets, praying for justice for everyone involved. Prayer and confidence in God—what a concept! No matter what the outcome of this pitched battle is, the citizens of this small city have seen what can happen when a few band together in the cause of justice. They may not change minds, but they have changed not a few hearts.

Turning to God

Dear Lord, sometimes I struggle with a world at odds with your word. Help me persevere and be a sign of strength to any and all who need me.

Thought in Action

Today and every day, let's find ways to be signs of good news and God's love to everyone we meet.

Friday
of the First Week

Psalm 130

With the Lord there is steadfast love.

Exploring the verses

My soul waits, and in his word I hope.

When I pray "thy will be done," do I mean it? Or do I place conditions and qualifications on the phrase?

With the Lord there is steadfast love, and with him is great power to redeem.

Would I recognize the deep joy of God's love if I felt it?

Reflection

I lost my parents within a period of eighteen months, first my father, then my mother. At the time my mother died, a friend wrote to say how hard it must have been to undergo two such monumental losses in so short a time. But the time had not seemed short to me—my father went quickly and unexpectedly, while my mother lingered through surgeries, strokes, and the loss of awareness.

When my mother lay in her final coma, I prayed that she would get better, that she would return to sensibility, that she would know me. Then as the days went on, I prayed that she would die, so that she would be released from the prison her body had become, so that she could join my father as she so clearly seemed to want to do. Finally I prayed that God's will would be done, whatever it was, whatever it might mean. It was shortly after that that she died.

I certainly don't think that was a deliberate sequence on God's part to get me to trust in God's mercy and love—I really don't think God plays games like that with us. But I did have some lessons to learn about relying on God's will, not my own.

I have come to believe that when you say "thy will be done" and you really mean it, God's peace will surround you and guide you along. Even if we can't perceive it, it is there, and we'll receive it nonetheless.

Turning to God

Dear Lord, I pray for all those in pain. Be with them as you have always been with me, even when I didn't acknowledge your goodness and abiding presence. Help me to be a light in their darkness.

Thought in Action

Let's be mindful of those around us in unspeakable pain, and help them know God's mercy and love through our presence.

Saturday
of the First Week

Psalm 119

Do not utterly forsake me.

Exploring the verses

O, that my ways may be steadfast in keeping your statutes!

In my quest to do God's will, do I stop grasping at perfection and enjoy small moments of progress?

Happy are those...who seek him with their whole heart.

Is doing God's will something other-centered for me, or do I tend to enjoy most the tasks that will bring me glory?

Reflection

Well, it's taken some years, but I have finally realized that today's psalm, with its "Happy are they" refrain is not, after all, a psalm of envy. Instead, this is a psalm of great hope. "Happy are they whose way is blameless," yes—and we have the chance to be blameless, too.

The wonderful good news is that God gives us credit for effort, not just achievement. We as a people are so goal-oriented that we can't often relax and enjoy the moments of working toward the goal. All that seems to matter is the end result. But, as I've said to my son when badgering him to work on a history fair project, it's the gathering of the research, the writing of the paper, and the unmatchable experience of learning new things that make a project worthwhile, not an award at the end. Blue ribbons are a nice validation, but if that's all you're working toward, it's a pretty hollow experience if you don't win (come to think of it, even if you do!).

God's mercy and goodness are bolstering us up always. As a wise friend said to me years ago, "We may not know what God's will is, but if we act as if we are doing God's will, if we act in the confidence that what we are doing is what God wants us to be doing, then we are." I have always considered that God's voice speaking to me, and giving me great hope.

Turning to God

Dear Lord, help me to see you always and everywhere, guiding me and helping me to do your will. Let me bring your light to others.

Thought in Action

Let's pause long enough today and every day to thank God for God's abiding presence.

Second Sunday of Lent (A)

Psalm 33

Let your steadfast love, O Lord, be upon us, even as we hope in you.

Exploring the verses

Truly the eye of the Lord is on those who fear him.

How often is my belief merely lip-service? Have I ever really been tested in my faith?

The earth is full of the steadfast love of the Lord.

Do I really believe this? Do I show it by proclaiming my faith proudly and recklessly, not stopping to count the cost?

Reflection

There are times when it is almost impossible to find comfort and solace in faith. When we've just lost our job, or our car has been repossessed, or the alimony and child support payments are late again, and the water company has turned off the water, our cries to God for attention can seem fruitless and frustrating.

I have a friend who has been the victim of great personal injustice. She has every reason to be angry at the system (and she is), to be outraged at those who are doing her dirt (she is, but she tempers this with praying for them), to be on the warpath for revenge (she isn't). When we talk, I preach righteous vengeance, legal recourse, not letting the children see their father until debts are paid. She answers me calmly. Yes, things are at a bad pass, and she will consult her attorney, but at the same time there are thousands of things that happen to her each day that reveal God's love to her. To deprive her children's father of their presence punishes everyone involved—she has too finely honed a sense of justice and fair play to use their children as a weapon. She believes that God will see her through, and, because of her stalwart witness, I believe it, too. In her equanimity and serenity she puts me to shame. But, as we are both God's children, she also gives me great hope.

Turning to God

Dear Lord, help me to find the balance between justice and mercy. Help me bring your light to others as a beacon of hope, not as the torch of vengeance.

Thought in Action

Today, let's try to strengthen our faith, and find ways to make it come alive for others.

Second Sunday of Lent (B)

Psalm 116

I kept my faith.

Exploring the verses

O Lord, I am your servant.

Do my daily actions brand me as the servant of the Lord or as the servant of the world?

You have loosed my bonds.

Have I ever really felt the boundless freedom that comes from following God with conviction and purpose?

Reflection

"Precious in the sight of the Lord is the death of his faithful ones." What does it take to be a faithful one these days? And how do we manifest it in our daily lives? Growing up, I felt I had the best of both worlds. My father was Catholic, my mother a Disciple of Christ. Every Sunday Daddy and I went off to Mass while Mommy slept in (except on those rare occasions when Daddy had the flu, and Mommy would take me to church. I remember coaxing her to kneel, and her gentle but firm refusals.).

It was Daddy who used to take me over to Barclay Street in lower Manhattan to check out all the religious goods stores, and I used to come home with handfuls of holy cards, and lives of the saints. It was Mommy who chauffeured me to school each day, and made sure I was up on my holy days of obligation. It was Daddy who used to open his missal to pray quietly in the mornings before the rest of us were up. It was Mommy who took care of my aunt, Daddy's sister, when she came to live with us after a devastating stroke, and couldn't manage the most basic functions of life.

I saw faith and commitment on both sides. And I like to think I have learned and grown in faith from both their examples. Each in their way was one of God's faithful ones, and I have no doubt that they are both walking joyfully in the land of the living.

Turning to God

Dear Lord, keep me mindful of the joy of serving you, and help me remember the example of those who have gone before me.

Thought in Action

Let's accomplish one task today purely and simply for God's glory.

Second Sunday of Lent (C)

Psalm 27

Wait for the Lord; be strong,
and let your heart take courage.

Exploring the verses

Do not hide your face from me.

If I have rarely been aware of God's presence in my life, have I ever been aware of God's absence?

You have been my help.

Have I ever really tried to turn things over to God, to ask for God's help, and been ready to accept it however God chooses to send it?

Reflection

"The Lord is my light and my salvation; whom shall I fear? The Lord is the stronghold of my life; of whom shall I be afraid?" These are courageous words, spoken with a conviction and a certainty that I envy greatly.

In my own life, I'm much more skeptical. It's not that I don't think God can handle the job, it's just that I'm sure God has a lot more important things to do than pay attention to me.

And yet, there are those words, calm and insistent, about waiting, trusting, having confidence, being strong and steadfast.

I have a very good friend who is a constant reminder to me of God's clear and unflagging devotion to each and every one of us. No matter what life hands her, she accepts it with equanimity and good grace. She fights for justice for those who are mistreated, and she is unafraid to voice her opinions, even if they go against the grain. She takes her responsibilities as a citizen, mother, wife, friend, and person of faith very seriously indeed, and her faith inspires and informs everything she does. She is truly a gift to know, and a vibrant example to follow. I once asked her what her favorite Scripture passage was. She replied with the words that begin this psalm: "The Lord is my light and my salvation; whom should I fear?" I envy such clearmindedness and confidence—and I hope even a little of it rubs off on me!

Turning to God

Dear Lord, thank you for the examples you send me each day of your love.

Thought in Action

Let's try today to be better witnesses of God's justice and compassion.

Monday
of the Second Week

Psalm 79

Let your compassion come speedily to meet us.

Exploring the verses

According to your great power preserve those doomed to die...then we will give thanks to you forever.

Sound familiar? How much of my prayer is bargaining with God? If you do this, then I will...? Who's better at keeping the bargain?

From generation to generation we will recount your praise.

Do I ever pause to consider what a great miracle it is that God loves me not in spite of my humanity but because of it?

Reflection

I am always guilty of knowing better than God how things should be ordered. When my son needed his third heart operation, I made it a quest, a cause, to storm the gates of heaven on his behalf. I boldly decided to ask for a miracle, that he be spared the experience for a third time.

I got my miracle—in a way that demonstrated God's great compassion, not to mention sense of humor. When it was time for my son's next checkup, the surgeon told us it could wait another year. In my nearsightedness, all I had been praying for was that it wouldn't happen *then*. At Mass one year later, as his checkup approached, I asked God for a sign. No sooner had I asked than the organist began to play Bach's "God's Time Is the Best."

People tell me this reliance on coincidence isn't the best way to witness a deep and abiding faith. They may be right, but for me, those incidents were God's way of taking me aside and assuring me that all would be well—in God's time and in God's way, not my own.

Turning to God

Dear Lord, grant me the humility to accept your will as graciously as you offer your love to me. Let me be a sign of witness, not contradiction, of your tenderness and grace.

Thought in Action

Today (and every day), let's remember to thank God for something. Let's also try to find blessings in disguise.

Tuesday
of the Second Week

Psalm 50

Not for your sacrifices do I rebuke you.

Exploring the verses

To those who go the right way I will show the salvation of God.

Do I try to model Christ in my actions every day, no matter what they are?

What right have you to recite my statutes, or take my covenant on your lips? For you hate discipline, and you cast my words behind you.

Do I embrace God's word fully, or do I constantly find more comfortable loopholes and qualifications?

Reflection

"Think you that I am like yourself?" asks God in this psalm. I fear our short answer is often "yes." We are always confusing our abilities and talents with the incredible and unapproachable mystery that is God's love and care for us.

We observe the externals of the law—we go to Mass, we remember our envelopes, we even make a more than halfhearted stab at a genuine sign of peace (especially if we know the people around us). But we confuse our ways with God's. We define the Godhead in our own woefully inadequate terms. We create God in our image and likeness.

But God does not want our ostentatious displays of piety, our keeping ahead of the Joneses when it comes to contributing to annual appeals and rubbing elbows with high-up chancery officials. No, "Those who bring thanksgiving as their sacrifice honor me," says God.

Look beyond the handshake at the sign of peace and look into the eyes of the one whose hand you're holding. What manifestation of Jesus do you see in that person? How hard is it for you to look?

If we all started to pay attention to the Christ in one another, God would indeed be glorified in our midst.

Turning to God

Dear Lord, open my eyes to see you in everyone I meet. Let me reverence you and praise you by my love for others. Keep me honest in your sight and make me a worthy disciple.

Thought in Action

Today let's make each word from our lips a song of praise or a word of comfort.

Wednesday
of the Second Week

Psalm 31

My times are in your hand.

Exploring the verses

I hear the whispering of many.

Do people seek me out for advice and counsel? Or do people run the other way when they see me approach?

Into your hand I commit my spirit.

How willing am I to make a leap of faith—and mean it?

Reflection

It's not hard to spot the people for whom this prayer is a reality. Look at the strong courage and conviction in the eyes of Oscar Romero, the serenity and joy of God's presence in Thomas Merton, the radiance of God shining through the dying Cardinal Bernardin, the pure and naked love of Mother Teresa, the ferocity of the quest for justice in Dorothy Day. Each of these people in their own ways put themselves completely at God's service. Whatever God wanted, whatever risks that calling entailed, these people embraced—some joyfully and immediately, some after a great deal of searching and discernment.

Okay—these models are pretty much taken for granted today. It's easy to spot sanctity at a remove. But what about in your own life, in your own neighborhood, in your own parish? Have you ever watched people in the communion line? Some are tired, some are bored, but some are radiant with an inner light and peace that shouts of God's presence within them. There are teachers in my son's school who inspire me every day to live as they do, constantly and unstintingly offering unconditional love and encouragement to the children in their charge. These are people you go to when your own batteries need recharging—and they always have enough of God's energy to share.

All it takes for God to use us is to make the leap of faith that puts us securely in God's hands.

Turning to God

Dear Lord, help me recognize you in all the wonderful people you put in my life. And help me reflect your light, too.

Thought in Action

Let us try to live just one day in complete service of the Lord. Let's try to make it a habit!

Thursday of the Second Week

Psalm 1

The way of the wicked will perish.

Exploring the verses

Happy are those who do not follow the advice of the wicked...

Do I greatly enjoy gossip and rumors about other people?

...or sit in the seat of scoffers.

If I find myself in a situation where stories are being spread, do I walk away, or do I listen silently, contributing with my complacency?

Reflection

I spent a couple of hours this morning volunteering at my son's school, filling in for a teacher who had an early morning meeting. By the time I left the building, I had mediated disputes, done a bunch of recordkeeping—attendance, milk money, hot lunch money, etc.—and shepherded the kids to and from morning prayer in the church. (And of course *none* of these kids would *ever* take advantage of a substitute!) In the midst of this I heard more rumors and gossip than could fill the pages of all the supermarket tabloids put together—from the adults!

There just seems to be something in us that enjoys the foibles of others. And, let's face it, in our own minds, there's just about nothing we couldn't improve, given half the chance. (How many times have you heard someone say, "When I get to heaven, I'm really going to have to speak to God about..."? Ever said it yourself?) None of this is surprising, and I'm not even trying to assign blame. My point is that all of this is human nature, pure and simple. How amazing it is to hear God's faith in us when we've done nothing, absolutely nothing, to deserve it.

Maybe if God thinks so well of us, we could start thinking better of ourselves. Then dissecting the problems and difficulties of others wouldn't be half as appealing as the attempts we might make to offer help and comfort. It's a thought.

Turning to God

Dear Lord, help me remember that there's always more than one side to a story, and that someone involved is always in pain. Let me be a worthy servant, and not just an accomplice in crime.

Thought into Action

Let's find one thing today that we can do to support someone in pain.

Friday
of the Second Week

Psalm 105

The word of the Lord kept testing him.

Exploring the verses

He had sent a man ahead of them.

Do I consider myself sent by God? If I did, would I treat others differently?

His feet were hurt with fetters, his neck was put in a collar of iron; until what he had said came to pass.

How often do I let "wait-and-see" attitudes determine my course in dealing with others? How much proof do I need before I believe?

Reflection

You know the story of Joseph, the man of the many-colored coat. His brothers were so jealous of him they sold him into slavery, and went home telling their father, Jacob, that Joseph was dead. Years later, during a time of great famine, Jacob's sons came to Egypt, to the Pharaoh's court. Who should be there in a position of great authority but their brother Joseph?! Joseph could have used his influence to condemn his brothers. Instead, he treated them all with compassion and mercy.

We are people sent by God. Some of us write, some of us preach, some of us teach, some parent, some doctor and nurse us, some work in factories, some work at the checkout counter. Whatever we do for a living, we are always in a position to spread God's word.

Each and every one of us is uniquely gifted to be a living witness of God's goodness here on earth. The story goes that some monks were having a terrible time getting along with one another until a sage told them that God was in their midst. The monks, not knowing which of them was the living God, started treating one another with respect and love. We can do no less.

Turning to God

Dear Lord, make us instruments of your peace. Let our gifts be at your service so that we can let your light shine for others. Help us to recognize you in others and seize every chance to praise your name.

Thought into Action

Today and every day, let's make a concerted effort to witness Christian love and compassion with all those we meet.

Saturday
of the Second Week

Psalm 103

As far as the east is from the west, so far he removes our transgressions from us.

Exploring the verses

Bless the Lord, O my soul, and all that is within me, bless his holy name.

How can I be a more effective disciple?

Nor will he keep his anger for ever.

Can I try to be more like Christ—forgiving and forgetting?

Reflection

Here is the good news pure and simple. We are sinners; God sent Jesus to redeem us by his life, death, and resurrection; after such a sacrifice, our transgressions are forgiven—and *forgotten*. No grudges, no "golden moments" hidden away in memory banks to be brought out as ammunition at the next fight, no recriminations. Indeed we should be blessing the Lord at all times, every moment of the day, for the graciousness, mercy, and love we have been shown.

When the full impact of what God's unconditional love means hits me, I want to give it back—I want to be of the greatest service and aid I can to everyone who might need my help. It doesn't take long, though, for me to feel put upon, to feel taken advantage of, to feel patronized. I want to keep my witness to God's love pure, but it is always tainted by the hazards of being human.

Here's the miracle: God knows this, and God understands. And God loves us anyhow. God loves us for trying. God loves us when we fail. GOD LOVES US.

How can this not be good news? How can this not make us want to strive to be ardent disciples, bringing God's light and love to others? God will give us the ability, if we only trust in God's goodness to make it so.

Turning to God

Dear Lord, help me to see you in the faces of everyone I meet. Help me to spread your good news of love and light and joy. Let me be a comfort to those in distress, let me give without thinking of the cost, and let me praise and bless you with everything I say and do.

Thought in Action

Let's try harder to find God in others, the God who is waiting for our welcome.

Third Sunday of Lent (A)

Psalm 95

O come, let us sing to the Lord.

Exploring the verses

Let us come into his presence with thanksgiving.

Do I appreciate the gifts of God's kindness and compassion? Do I show this by sharing them with others?

Your ancestors tested me…though they had seen my work.

Do I test God's goodness and mercy? How can I learn to trust God more?

Reflection

It is perhaps easier to be open to God's message on Sunday than on any other day of the week. When we share in the Eucharist with our parish family we are surrounded by a community of like-minded souls (we like to think). Carrying God's message out through the church doors to the people in our workaday world is the real test.

Speaking of tests—God asks us in the psalm not to harden our hearts, but to be open to let the love of God enter and make us whole. Are we ready to accept that kind of love? It is completely unconditional, but that doesn't mean it comes without responsibility. God's love is revealed in this world by the way we treat one another—and that means *everybody*, not just the people we like, or the ones who are nice to us, or the ones we want to impress. It means taking a moment to acknowledge that the cashier at the checkout line may be having just as bad a day as you are, or noticing that a coworker seems distracted or withdrawn. It means reaching out to others with the fullness of our being—being aware, going through life with our eyes open and our arms ready to embrace. We worship God daily by bringing God to others. This love is powerful stuff!

Turning to God

Dear Lord, thank you for always reminding me of your love. Please keep on reminding me, so that I'll have all the strength I need to carry the joy of your word to others.

Thought in Action

Let's be a sign of God's love and light in the world today and every day.

Third Sunday of Lent (B)

Psalm 19

Making wise the simple.

Exploring the verses

The fear of the Lord is pure.

How often do I interpret "fear of God" as mistrust and aversion, instead of awe and wonder?

The commandment of the Lord is clear.

Do I take time each day to pause and ponder what God might be calling me to do? Would my day be different if I did?

Reflection

A friend of mine made an agreement with her middle-school son that if his grades slipped, he would have restricted access to his Nintendo. The son agreed amicably, and all seemed well—until one of his grades took a decided slide.

My friend imposed the agreed-upon restriction. We could hear the uproar all the way across town! The bargaining, protests, and complaining went on for hours, my friend told me, but she stuck to her guns and insisted that she meant it when she said that studying came before playtime. Grudgingly the son complied, and the next report card showed improvement.

I'd like to say that everyone was pleased with this result. Unfortunately, the kid, being a kid, felt his "punishment" was unjust, unfair, and unconstitutional. The mother felt her dictum had been clear and not open to interpretation. The outcome was more than satisfying to Mom, but an unwilling admission of responsibility for the child.

I fear I face God this way nearly all the time. I bargain, I cajole, I make deals. The path before me couldn't be more clearly marked, yet I find all kinds of detours. May I take this psalm to heart!

Turning to God

Dear Lord, help me put myself in your hands, trust your plan, walk in your ways. Keep my focus straight and unwavering. Guide me ever to your side.

Thought in Action

Let's try to recognize one instance today where God is speaking to us—and let us respond without hesitation.

Third Sunday of Lent (C)

Psalm 103

The Lord is merciful and gracious.

Exploring the verses

For as the heavens are high above the earth, so great is his steadfast love.

Do I recognize and embrace the kindness of God revealed to me in so many ways every day?

Bless the Lord, O my soul, and all that is within me, bless his holy name.

How often do I bless the Lord, thank the Lord for all the goodness around me—at home, at work, in the eyes of those I love?

Reflection

A few years ago, a friend of mine asked me to take part in an ecumenical prayer service to show our community's solidarity with the people of Atlanta whose churches had been destroyed.

It was an amazing evening—there were Catholics, Bahai's, Jews, Unitarians, Lutherans, Congregationalists, Evangelicals, all raising our voices to God and proclaiming our trust and confidence in God's justice and mercy. We prayed for the victims, we prayed for the arsonists. We prayed to change ourselves that the world might change. At the end, a local choir sang "Our God Is an Awesome God," and the entire theatre where we were meeting erupted in sound. And I think all of us walked out of there somehow changed.

Whenever I hear this psalm, I think of that evening. I am reminded that God not only forgives all our sins, God redeems us. How can we repay this gift? God shows us how. We are crowned "with kindness and compassion," given the tools with which to go out into the world spreading the good news of salvation and mercy and peace.

When I remember to tune my soul to wonder, this psalm makes my heart sing.

Turning to God

Dear Lord, help me use your gifts of kindness and compassion to show your goodness to everyone I meet. Help me remember that you love and cherish all of us. No one is unimportant in your sight.

Thought in Action

Let's savor the words of this psalm and feel ourselves "crowned" with the confidence to be an effective disciple in the world.

Monday
of the Third Week

Psalm 42, NAB

Send forth your light and your fidelity.

Exploring the verses

When shall I go and behold the face of God? (NAB)

Are there people in my neighborhood, parish, family, who are
suffering rejection, misunderstanding, ostracism? How can I
bring the good news to them?

The God of my gladness and joy.

How often is God a part of my rejoicing? Or do I only
acknowledge my need for God when I am in pain?

Reflection

At one time or another, I bet we've all been people who question God's goodness, people who doubt their faith, people who see a different God revealed in practice than in preaching, people who are rejected and cast off by those who claim holiness and rectitude. It's a long, weary journey from the plaintive "whens" of the first part of this psalm to the confident "thens" of the second. And it's a sad fact that many of us never make it.

What can we do to spread good news into the lives of people whose longing has been replaced with bitterness, whose experience of God has been tempered way too much by their experience of life, whose reaching out for solace has been met with refusal and silence—even in our faith communities? We can pray for them, yes. Prayer is always a good idea. But more pointedly, we can walk with them on their way, be present to them as witnesses of a God who is greater, mightier, and more attentive than any institution could ever be.

We can be signs of unconditional love and forgiveness and mercy and justice. *When* we do these things, *then* we will be effective and shining witnesses of God's love and unlimited goodness.

Turning to God

Dear Lord, help me to bring light where there is darkness, acceptance and welcome where there is shame and despair, love and honor where there is hate and rejection. Let your good news shine through me.

Thought in Action

Let's do something today to turn somebody's *when* into a God-filled *then*.

Tuesday
of the Third Week

Psalm 25

Make me to know your ways, O Lord.

Exploring the verses

Lead me in your truth, and teach me.

Can I try to act as if I understand the incredible mercy of God?

He instructs sinners in the way.

Can I be a witness, however imperfectly, of such love?

Reflection

Today I found myself praying hard for a just and right outcome to an untenable situation. One of my friends is being treated unfairly and unjustly in her work for the church. I want to take her superiors to task, to remind them of their sacred calling to love and mercy. But, beneath a thin veil of secrecy, there are threats of negative consequences if any outside help is sought.

When I was praying I suddenly realized that I was praying, "Vengeance is mine, says the Lord, but let me have just a little bit, and let me make it stick so that they hurt!" All of a sudden it hit me like a bolt—justice is the Lord's, but I'm afraid that God is just too merciful to really exact a penalty from them. I want to be sure they squirm and tremble NOW. But God will forgive them; God is so full of compassion and mercy that he accepts our repentance whenever it's offered.

I can't pretend to understand mercy of this magnitude. Frankly, I can't let go of my own need to seek vengeance. I'm the one who needs the work; I'm the one who needs the understanding. I know God will guide me wisely and rightly in whatever quest I can make for justice for my friend, if I leave it in God's hands and ask only to be a humble and effective instrument of God's will.

But boy, just this once, would I ever like to write the script!

Turning to God

Dear Lord, help me do what is right, what will do the most good without inflicting harm. Let me put aside any notions of personal satisfaction and triumph I might be entertaining, and let me just be a pure vessel of your own mercy and justice.

Thought in Action

Today, let's find a situation that calls for justice, and work to see that justice is done—while tempered with mercy.

Wednesday
of the Third Week

Psalm 147

He blesses your children within you.

Exploring the verses

Praise your God, O Zion!

Do I stop for at least one moment each and every day and thank God for the gift of life—my own and the lives of all those I know and love?

He has not dealt thus with any other nation.

Do I believe I am somehow uniquely favored by God? Do I praise God's goodness in making each of his children unique?

Reflection

I am amazed every morning when my son staggers into the kitchen, eyes still half-closed. He's fourteen, and has outgrown me (nearly six feet tall and counting!). Daily it astonishes me that we see eye to eye physically—if not always emotionally. It wasn't that long ago that he was little enough to lift with one hand, then just tall enough to come up to his father's knee.

Michael is blessed in many ways—a keen mind, a great sense of humor, a sensitive and loving nature that still has enough room in it for mischief. Don't get me wrong—he's not perfect, but he is a constant joy.

I don't know of any force more powerful than that of parental love. Its ferocity is mindboggling. One day, when I was pondering this point at length, a new realization hit me. The way I love my son—the sure and certain knowledge that there is nothing he could ever do that would turn me against him—this is *exactly* the way God loves me, and you, and everyone. Flawed and imperfect as we are, we are still cherished as unique and important beings in God's eyes. If we really believe that, how can we not be filled with awe and wonder at our amazing God, and all the ways God speaks to us each day?! And what about this: if we started to share this conviction with others, might not the world become a kinder place?

Turning to God

Dear Lord, keep me filled with gratitude. When I consider the wonders you have done, my heart nearly bursts with joy and praise.

Thought in Action

Let's count our blessings, not list our grievances. Let's celebrate life, not wallow in misery. Let's advocate justice, not condone injustice.

Thursday
of the Third Week

Psalm 95

Let us make a joyful noise to him with songs of praise!

Exploring the verses

O come, let us worship and bow down.

Do I find something in each day to praise God for? Can I try to find something, if I don't do so now?

O, that today you would listen to his voice!

Can I find God in the silence as well as in the symphony?

Reflection

Are our prayers often (ever?) filled with this kind of jubilation tinged with the longing that everyone we meet will be filled with the same kind of joy? Have times of tribulation muted whatever joy we might have felt at one time?

Prayer is rarely as boisterously loud and unaffected as it is here. My prayers are often prayers of lament, of contrition, of petition. But there are moments, even hours or days, when my heart is full of an irrepressible joy, a joy that can't be contained. I want to share the good news of God's love and mercy always and everywhere. Those are golden moments, and moments to be treasured.

But here's a secret I've learned—in this psalm the Lord asks that we not harden our hearts. A very wise friend of mine pointed out that a heart has to be broken to open up enough to let God in. God is with us just as vibrantly and attentively in the moments when we feel most alone as when we are sure and confident of the rightness of God's universe.

Let us harden not our hearts—not to God, not to each other. Spreading joy is infectious. Give it a try. As with any of God's gifts shared with others, it will be returned a hundredfold.

Turning to God

Dear Lord, thank you for your presence in my life. Thank you for the goodness that you shower on me daily, even when I don't see it, or feel it, or acknowledge it. Make me a witness of your love to others so that your light will continue to shine.

Thought in Action

Today, let us try to hear the cry of the brokenhearted, and help them feel the warmth of God's love.

Friday
of the Third Week

Psalm 81

I hear a voice I had not known.

Exploring the verses

O Israel, if you would but listen to me.

Am I aware of how many ways God is speaking to me each and every day?

I would feed you with the finest of the wheat, and with honey from the rock I would satisfy you.

Would I be ashamed of myself if I tried to count God's daily blessings, and found myself showered with them, even on the days when I feel most beleaguered by life?

Reflection

This is one of the psalms that fills me, clueless disciple that I am, with great hope in God and God's goodness. The psalmist is the one who finds God's voice unfamiliar. And that confusion or misperception rings a familiar chord down the ages from then to now. How often do we hear God's voice? Perhaps we're looking for great events, or earth-shaking calamities, or even straining our ears to find out if the still small voice we just heard might be that of God.

While we are thus engaged, the wonder of God's universe is thundering around us, mighty as the majestic mountain peaks, and quiet and gentle as our baby's rapturous gurgles.

Yes, God carries on, walking with us, answering our prayers, in spite of all our attempts to test, to bargain, to curry favor—and managing withal not to hear, see, or feel God's presence. What wondrous love is this, indeed!

Turning to God

Dear Lord, help me to hear your voice. Do not let your voice be strange or unrecognizable to me. Let me hear you everywhere, and respond with gratitude and praise, spreading your message with everything I do.

Thought in Action

Let's try today to notice God's work in our world, and offer thanks.

Saturday
of the Third Week

Psalm 51

Wash me thoroughly from my iniquity.

Exploring the verses

Cleanse me from my sin.

Am I afraid of the commitment I'll be making if I truly desire to be washed thoroughly of guilt?

O Lord, open my lips, and my mouth will declare your praise.

Do I have the courage to trust that God will give me the strength I need?

Reflection

Once again Psalm 51 comes to remind us of what we are about. And it asks a lot of us.

Asking God to wash us thoroughly of our guilt means that we want a clean slate. But clean slates themselves are scary. What do we fill them with? Do we actually want to begin a new way of life, a life lived in the knowledge of right and wrong, a life dedicated to service and love, a life of unselfishness and compassion? Some of our flaws are cozy and comfortable—not to mention badges that people can identify us by. Can't we be washed just a little, or—like smokers using nicotine patches—can't we be weaned of our sinfulness?

I suppose that works for some people, as cutting down on booze seems to work for some heavy drinkers. But the cleaner the break, the sooner the new life can begin. We can trust that God will not leave us hanging without giving us the strength and courage to persevere in our new way of life, and to keep trying again and again.

It's hard not to fear the unknown. But if we allow ourselves to become new creations, we will be able to face our world on its own terms—we won't have to hide in the shadows or behind our defenses anymore. And that's really good news!

Turning to God

Dear Lord, wash me thoroughly from my guilt so that your light will shine clearly through me on everyone I meet.

Thought in Action

Let's remember to pray for our catechumens and candidates as they prepare for their own new beginnings.

Fourth Sunday of Lent (A)

Psalm 23

Surely goodness and mercy shall follow me all the days of my life.

Exploring the verses

He makes me lie down in green pastures.

How often do I take a break in my day to feel God breathing through me, refreshing me and giving me strength?

I fear no evil.

Is this something I truly believe? Can I think of times in my life when my faith was strong enough to proclaim this?

Reflection

Even if you've never opened a Bible, you've probably heard parts of this psalm somewhere along the way. Its simple message of conviction, trust, confidence, and quiet joy—as fresh and vibrant now as when it was first sung—has brought consolation and hope to people for thousands of years.

Imagine that! These very thoughts—composed, tradition tells us, by the same poet who composed Psalm 51—have lasted through destructions of temples, the birth, death, and resurrection of the Savior, persecutions, schisms, and countless translations, interpretations, and musical settings. When a message is important enough for us to remember, God is going to make sure it doesn't get lost!

God wants us to know that we are not alone, that God is beside us, no matter where our journey through life takes us, or how much hardship we face. We need not fear; we can rely confidently on God's presence with us.

This is a hard message to share with people suffering the loss of a loved one, or some other life tragedy. Yet this is the psalm that we hear most in times of sorrow as well as of joy. It's up to us to reflect our own confidence and trust in God's mercy and love with all we meet. When we spread the word, we keep the message alive!

Turning to God

Dear Lord, I trust in your call, and have confidence that you will use me well. With you to guide me, I know I won't let you down!

Thought in Action

Let's try to live our lives today confidently, without fear, trusting in God's care—and help others do the same.

Fourth Sunday of Lent (B)

Psalm 137

How could we sing the Lord's song in a foreign land?

Exploring the verses

By the rivers of Babylon—there we sat down and there we wept.

Do I often feel discouraged, cut off from the Lord? What would bring me back?

Our tormentors asked for mirth.

How "mirthful" can I be in the face of the daily grind? How much of my "mirth" is just coping?

Reflection

There are times when I am truly satisfied in my work. My time is productive, I have pages to show for my effort, and there's still time left over to catch up on e-mail, or knitting, or just watching an episode of a soap opera.

Then there's most of the time—when deadlines are flexible for everyone else but me, when a ringing phone or a suddenly announced half-day at school throws my schedule into a tizzy, when one project has to be set completely aside to make room for another.

How I respond to this psalm depends completely on my mood and what's going on in my life. Sometimes I consider the "tormentors" those (very good!) friends of mine who remind me how lucky I am to work at home, who remind me to count my blessings, or to regain my focus and just get the job DONE instead of complaining about it. They have an important message to teach me—and I should listen!

Other times, I can't help but sit alongside the riverbank with the sad refugees and refuse to sing. Then the "tormentors" are all those (very good!) friends of mine who remind me how lucky I am to work at home, who remind me to count my blessings, or to regain my focus and get the job DONE instead of complaining about it. They have an important message to teach me—but I won't listen.

As always, God speaks to me in these words and through others. How receptive I am to the message is up to me.

Turning to God

Dear Lord, help me to listen for you and to you. Keep me out of my own way and open to your voice.

Thought into Action

Let's stop griping and start singing!

Fourth Sunday of Lent (C)

Psalm 34

O magnify the Lord with me.

Exploring the verses

This poor soul cried, and was heard by the Lord.

How often when "poor souls" around me call out do I hear and respond? What can I do to be more aware of the "cry of the poor"?

I will bless the Lord at all times.

Do I spend more time blessing God for God's goodness, or cursing my fate? How can I be more open to rejoicing?

Reflection

"I believe...I believe..." Anyone familiar with the holiday classic *Miracle on 34th Street* will recognize these words as those of little Susan Walker right before she spies the house she longed for, and her dreams come true. So that nice Mr. Kringle *was* Santa Claus after all! In *Pollyanna*, the little girl who brings so much joy to so many wants a doll of her very own. One of the people she has helped makes sure she wins a doll at the local fair, and the look on Pollyanna's face is one of pure awe and wonder.

These are wonderful, heartwarming moments because they speak of dreams fulfilled, and wishes granted. This psalm, which we hear often during Lent, is meant to bolster our belief as well. There are times when it is easy to "glory in the Lord" so much that God's radiance shines forth from us to touch others. At other times, though, it's just so much whistling in the dark—hoping that by proclaiming confidence, confidence will grow.

I'm reminded of another cinematic moment—in *The King and I*, when Anna, newly arrived to teach the king's children in Siam, is trying to reassure her son (and summon her own courage!) by whistling: "Make believe you're brave, and the trick will take you far.... You may be as brave as you make believe you are," she sings.

At times when our conviction is shaky, when we can't even remember what it might be like to have God on our side, let us remember the words of this beautiful psalm—and see if wishing just might not make it so!

Turning to God

Dear Lord, give me confidence to believe in your promise. Give me hope to bring your light to others.

Thought in Action

Let's act today "as if" we believe—and see if it makes a difference.

Monday
of the Fourth Week

Psalm 30

You have turned my mourning into dancing.

Exploring the verses

Weeping may linger for the night, but joy comes with the morning.

Am I sensitive to others' feelings and needs? Do I need to be more aware?

O Lord, be my helper!

When I am feeling down, alone, misunderstood, do I let the light of others in? Am I as eager to be ministered to as I am to minister?

Reflection

The idea that mourning can be turned into dancing is a hard sell for people caught in the grip of hardship, bereavement, depression, or addiction. Those caught in the grip of darkness and grief don't want pious platitudes from us. And, if we're honest with ourselves, we're more convinced (and convincing) at some moments than others when we share our own hope and encouragement. But by asserting God's goodness in the face of despair, by just being there as the deputy of God—our shoulders representing those of our waiting and compassionate God—we might be able to share the message that there is light at the end of the tunnel.

The good news is that God is waiting to dance right along with us. God wants us to share in the wonderful history of salvation. Each and every one of us who has been redeemed by Jesus' death has a part to play in this history.

We have to get used to the idea that joy should be our primary mode of being. Sharing God's love and light with others shouldn't be a burden but a privilege. Perhaps if we start approaching life with gratitude and awe, this will be easier for us. Just for today, give it a try.

Turning to God

Dear Lord, thank you for all the ways you allow joy to break through the chains of darkness. Help me to be a beacon of your light for everyone I meet.

Thought in Action

Let's try today to live as if we believe and rejoice in the good news. Let's also actively seek a chance to share the message.

Tuesday
of the Fourth Week

Psalm 46

Come, behold the works of the Lord.

Exploring the verses

The Lord of hosts is with us.

Do I reverence and celebrate God each day?

God is our refuge and strength, a very present help in trouble.

Are my eyes open to see the amazing works God is doing?

Reflection

A few years ago, I had the immense pleasure of working with a man on a collection of his writings about how he saw the world, and what God meant to him. He was an amazing person—in the course of his life (he was "in his ninetieth year"), he had taught astronomy, been a world-class yachtsman, had run a ballet company, and was an ardent lover of music, God, women's basketball, and life. His thirst for knowledge and understanding was endless and enthusiastic. He relished greeting and getting to know all kinds of people—everyone had some important message to share, and he was eager to hear it. His favorite word was "Behold!" He felt this word was exactly appropriate for the awe and wonder with which we should approach God's creation.

He believed that in the right light, and if your eyes are attuned to such things, the most mundane daily objects can take on a patina, a certain dignity and quiet beauty, of placement, of color, of light interaction. All of this is part of God's amazing and wondrous creation, and it's all just waiting for us to see, enjoy, and celebrate.

My friend died before his reflections were published, and the world is dimmed without his presence. I have no doubt, though, that he is glorying in the vision of heaven that he saw so clearly here on earth. I treasure his memory, and try to see life each day with eyes of gratitude and wonder.

Turning to God

Dear Lord, keep me aware of your presence and guidance. Make me a cheerful and capable disciple of your good news.

Thought in Action

Today, let's try to think of just five things that reflect God's goodness and beauty—and see if we can think of more!

Wednesday of the Fourth Week

Psalm 145

The Lord is near to all who call on him,
to all who call on him in truth.

Exploring the verses

The Lord upholds all who are falling, and raises up all who are bowed down.

Am I aware of God's infinite goodness even once in every day?

The Lord is good to all, and his compassion is over all that he has made.

Am I aware that I am one of those "all"? Do I rejoice in this knowledge?

Reflection

Do the ringing words of this psalm get your soul singing? Or do you find some of it uncomfortable to hear?

How often when we call upon the Lord do we do so in praise, gratitude, or thanksgiving? Or are we more likely to call upon the Lord strictly in times of our own neediness and our misguided sense of what praying is about? Thomas Merton put it well: "What is the use of praying if at the very moment of prayer we have so little confidence in God that we are busy planning our own kind of answer to our prayer?"

Calling on God *in truth* means letting God be God, realizing and accepting that God's ways are not our ways, that God may very well be working for our good in ways we could never imagine—in our most impassioned prayers.

At the same time, however, even when our prayers are skewed to our own personal advantage, God understands. God knows this is all part of that amazing human nature he created—and allowed his Son to share. The Lord is good to all. That includes you and me and everyone else on earth. Flawed and imperfect as we are, God is there beside us, enjoying us, and showering us with goodness. That's a remarkable promise.

Turning to God

Dear Lord, help me shine with your light. Let your compassion be mine so that others will see your goodness and love.

Thought in Action

Let's examine today whether, in our relationship with God, we confuse who is made in whose image. Let's bask in God's love and not merely seek favors.

Thursday
of the Fourth Week

Psalm 106

They exchanged the glory of God for the image of an ox that eats grass.

Exploring the verses

They forgot God, their Savior.

Do I forget God in the hustle and bustle of daily life?

God's wondrous works in the land of Ham, and awesome deeds by the Red Sea.

Do I try to remember each day all the blessings that surround me, or do I continually concentrate on everything that goes wrong?

Reflection

The psalmist's description of the Israelites in the desert sounds withering enough. But it gets worse. This people has forgotten all that God has done for them. God is ready to destroy them, as in the days of Noah, but Moses asks God to be merciful. And, for the sake of the just, God obliges.

Imagine those ingrates! God helps them escape from slavery and gets ready to offer them the promised land. But they're impatient and they lose heart, and they start to let their minds and purpose wander. Before you know it, they are worshiping other gods. Sound familiar?

We exchange glory for the quick fix every day of the week in varying degrees. Some days we succeed better at remembering what really matters. But at other times we're only too happy to overspend, or succumb to the Sunday morning lazies, or display our brilliantly cutting wit at another's expense. In so many ways we ignore or forget the great mercy and love God showers upon us, which it is our privilege to witness.

Lent is a wonderful time for taking stock not just of our personal shortcomings, but of our limitless opportunities to give service to God. A smile instead of a sneer will get the ball rolling. And sometimes it's the tiniest gesture that has the greatest effect.

Turning to God

Dear Lord, give me the strength, courage, and wisdom to seek your will in all things, and to practice it in everything I do. Let me not forget you, and let me worship you even in the imperfection of my attempts.

Thought in Action

Let's try today to reveal God's blessings to others—and mean it.

Friday
of the Fourth Week

Psalm 34

The Lord redeems the life of his servants; none of those who take refuge in him will be condemned.

Exploring the verses

Many are the afflictions of the righteous.

Do I let God be God, or do I demand signs that I can understand of God's action in my life?

The eyes of the Lord are on the righteous, and his ears are open to their cry.

How often does my idea of justice fail to mesh with God's?

Reflection

Yes! we want to cry, yes!, let the Lord be my vindication. Let me see the mighty works of the Lord as the evildoers are confronted, and remembrance of them is destroyed upon the earth. Then I will know for sure that God hears the cry of the just and delivers them from their distress. Then I will be certain that the Lord is close to the brokenhearted, that those crushed in spirit are saved. I will be confident that the Lord will deliver me from all my troubles.

It doesn't work that way, of course. We are our own worst enemies when it comes to facing God. God reaches out to us with open arms, with tender love and compassion. We demand instead that God punish the wicked and rain down wrath upon those who have hurt us.

Now righteous anger is fine. Fighting for justice is an important part of who we are. But vengeance is not an appropriate response for an all-loving God. We do ourselves dishonor when we ask it. God has promised to deal with evildoers—in God's way, not ours. Bear in mind that God's action may very well be to forgive, and to welcome our enemies with open arms. Who are we to whittle God's majesty and power down to petty human paybacks and revenge? Eye has not seen and ear has not heard what God has in store.

Turning to God

Dear Lord, even in the face of rejection and unfairness, let me know your comfort and your stalwart presence, and let this be enough for me.

Thought in Action

Today, let's take some time to consider that God will be as merciful to our enemies as God, we hope, will be to us.

Saturday
of the Fourth Week

Psalm 7

You who test the minds and hearts, O righteous God.

Exploring the verses

Save me from all my pursuers, and deliver me.

When I seek justice, have I thought of all sides of the question?

God who saves the upright of heart.

How "upright" is my heart? Or does my sense of rightness apply only to myself?

Reflection

There it is—right in the middle of this psalm: the phrase that sounds a cautionary chord: "you who test the minds and hearts, O righteous God." We may think we know what justice is and how to achieve it, but it is God who has the final say. God is a God of justice, a God who so believes in our essential goodness and who so completely loves us and who so deeply wants us to partake of divine justice and mercy that God sent his own and only Son to die and rise for us, to redeem us all. That Jesus, one like us in everything but sin, should be sacrificed for the likes of us doesn't sound like justice at all. It sounds like the highest form of foolishness. It sounds obscene. It is. Yet this is our just God. God so loved us that he has already passed judgment by sending Jesus to die for us. Even the wicked have a chance to be redeemed, if they will only respond to the invitation.

This is justice in God's terms. We all merit it, we are all entitled to it, and there are no evildoers who are not ultimately beautiful in God's eyes.

This kind of all-encompassing justice gives us, with our petty human definitions of the concept, a lot to think about—and a lot to emulate.

Turning to God

Dear Lord, keep me holy and blameless in your sight. In an unjust world, let me be a beacon of justice, mercy, and love. Let me be your capable and willing ambassador, and an eager evangelist of your incomparably good news.

Thought into Action

Today, let's pray for our oppressors, for all those who do us wrong, that they might see the light of mercy and compassion shining just out of reach—and let our actions help them to reach it.

Fifth Sunday of Lent (A)

Psalm 130

Out of the depths, I cry to you.

Exploring the verses

There is forgiveness with you.

Do I live my life joyously in the knowledge that I am saved? Do I share that joy with others?

In his word I hope.

Do I trust God and God's will for me? Or do I try to order the universe according to my design?

Reflection

We like to think our parishes are places of comfort and security, where we can be free and feel at home, warts and all. Sad to say, that may not be the case—at least in my (limited) experience. I've heard more hurtful gossip at parish bake sales and communion breakfasts than I ever do in the workaday world. And not just tale-telling, but malicious, character-assassinating salvos about other people's worthiness to even be a part of our community—moral judgments that should properly be left to our merciful, all-loving God.

I'm certainly no saint, but as I get older, and, I hope, wiser, I find it easier and easier to stay away from the "in crowd." Their criteria for acceptance are way too steep for me. I'm always surprised at the eagerness with which people want to share the most intimate personal details of people they barely know— people who aren't celebrities, but people we see each week, share peace with, receive Christ's body and blood from.

I praise God daily for the mercy and love that are showered down on all of us clueless creatures. If God marked our iniquity, surely we'd be toast. As it is, each day God gives us another chance to reach out rather than strike down, to be a source of light and not darkness, to get out of our own way and let ourselves be guided by good, not hurtful, news.

Turning to God

Dear Lord, it's so easy to give in and follow the crowd. Give me the courage and strength to strike out on your path, and invite others along.

Thought in Action

Today, let's try to notice if there's someone hurting whom we can embrace with welcome, or someone "outside" whom we can invite in.

Fifth Sunday of Lent (B)

Psalm 51

Sustain in me a willing spirit.

Exploring the verses

Put a new and right spirit within me.

Am I actually willing to be a part of God's plan? Or do I spend more time trying to follow my own agenda?

Then I will teach transgressors your ways, and sinners will return to you.

Do I really believe that by witnessing God's goodness everywhere—at work, at school, at home—that I really make any kind of difference in our world?

Reflection

When my son was younger, I did a lot of volunteering on the playground at his school. Most of the time things went smoothly—just the ordinary skinned knees or someone cutting in line or someone taking too long a pitching turn at kickball. Occasionally, though, the kids would act up in the lunchroom, and the volunteers in there would ask that we subtract recess time so that the kids would learn to behave better.

Well, in the wintertime we "outside moms" didn't want the kids just standing around, so we devised all kinds of ways to march around the perimeter of the schoolyard and the school grounds so that they would get their exercise, none of us would freeze, but we would still technically be in the business of exacting recompense. We actually had fun doing this, thinking up new patterns to walk, trying to surprise the kids. Once my family and I were in Ossining, NY, in an area overlooking Sing-Sing prison. Several prisoners were being marched around the prison yard for exercise. "Look, Mom," my son exclaimed, "Recess!" (So what, after all, were our little marches proving?)

Thank God that we are given all these new chances to correct ourselves—with humor, with love, and with grace. All we have to do is ask God, and the grace will be provided for us. What a gift!

Turning to God

Dear Lord, let me glory in the mystery of your love. Let me be cleansed of my sin so that I may shine more brightly in your name.

Thought in Action

Let's stop today, count to ten, take a deep breath—whatever it takes, to put ourselves in God's presence to do God's work with a clean and constant heart.

Fifth Sunday of Lent (C)

Psalm 126

The Lord has done great things for us.

Exploring the verses

We rejoiced.

Again in this penitential season we hear about rejoicing. How many more hints does God have to drop before I get the message?

May those who sow in tears reap with shouts of joy.

How often have I heard this phrase and dismissed it as pious nonsense? How might I change my heart to embrace it?

Reflection

There are people who say that I make Pollyanna look like a grouch, that I'm so cheerful it's disgusting. Okay, sometimes I lay it on a little thick (you'd be surprised what a good irritant bonhomie can be in the right circumstances!). For the most part, though, I don't use joy as a weapon. Seeing the glass half full comes easily to me. I would much rather laugh than cry. I would rather kill with kindness than wither with disdain. I am, I think, just wired for joy.

This isn't to say that my life has been one merry song. I face battles every day against injustice done to my family and friends. I fight for honesty in a world that deems it an outdated virtue. I struggle with compulsions and addictions that could overpower me if I let down my constant vigilance. It is this tension, in fact, that restores my soul, and makes me see the importance of embracing moments of rejoicing. Some mornings I glory with Pippa passing, singing with her: "God's in his heaven; all's right with the world." Other days, I mutter fiercely and defiantly Julian's mantra, "All will be well, and all will be well, and all manner of things will be well." But at the core of my soul, I do believe that all things work to God's glory—if we try to make that glory a reality in our daily world. God needs us to do God's work. Perhaps all we can do in a day is smile at someone we would otherwise dismiss. You never know what a sign of hope your mere presence can be for another.

Turning to God

Dear Lord, help me rejoice in your goodness even when it seems very far away. Hold me close when I can't find you.

Thought in Action

Today, let's think of all the things in our lives, right now, that bring us joy.

Monday
of the Fifth Week

Psalm 23

Surely goodness and mercy shall follow me
all the days of my life.

Exploring the verses

You anoint my head with oil; my cup overflows.

In my everyday life, do I try to be light for others?

Your rod and your staff—they comfort me.

Do I let God work through me, sharing love and compassion?

Reflection

What are we to make of the promise of this pastoral, peaceful psalm? I don't know anyone who can truly and triumphantly state that only goodness and kindness follow them. We seem to have troubles and heartache surrounding us, not just companioning us. I have found myself muttering the line quoted above through clenched teeth as I clawed my way through rush hour subway traffic, or faced rebuke or disapproval (sometimes justified, sometimes not).

I have prayed this psalm frequently, willing it to comfort me with its placid acceptance and sure conviction. I prayed it today before sitting to write this, and I think I got an inkling of what this promise can mean.

Goodness and kindness do follow us all the days of our life—if we are exuding them through our pores, and spreading them out to others. Have you ever noticed how some people can walk down a street with either a dark cloud or a brick wall nearly visible around them? On the other hand, I know that when faced with people who seem to me to be closest to Christ, I perceive a glow and peace about them that just radiate comfort.

Perhaps we're hiding too carefully within our shells. Perhaps goodness and kindness can be shields as strong and powerful as brick walls and clouds of doom. We are called to let our lights shine, and our good Shepherd has provided us with light in abundance.

Turning to God

Dear Lord, let me be light, so that you may shine more brightly in our world.

Thought in Action

Today, let's try to cut through the walls that others build up, and let some of their light out.

Tuesday
of the Fifth Week

Psalm 102

Do not hide your face from me on the day of my distress.

Exploring the verses

Answer me speedily on the day when I call.

How quick am I to blame God when things go wrong?

To hear the groans of the prisoners.

How quick am I to try and discern God's loving actions in the most unimaginable situations?

Reflection

After yesterday's peace and quiet certainty, today's psalm is like a slap in the face. The promise of God's goodness is to be read by "generations to come," when "future creatures" will praise the Lord. But the psalmist trusts in the glory to come, when the Lord "has regarded the prayer of the destitute and not despised their prayer."

We can take great solace from this achingly honest prayer. Even if we don't see the results of our prayers, even if we can't see any light at the end of our own personal tunnels, even if the world doesn't appear to be changing, our actions on God's behalf, even in just calling on God in prayer, have a salutary effect on the world. Like the drop of water that constantly drips on the same piece of rock, gradually eroding it away, each thing we do for good, each action we take in honesty and integrity, changes our world for the better, and helps to bring the kingdom closer. We lead by our example of humility and simplicity. We lead by our example of trust and confidence in our God.

We can and do make a difference each day of our lives, when we get out of the driver's seat of our own machinations, and let God take over and guide us. We can trust that God will be beside us in our darkest hour. And we can calmly and confidently witness that trust to others.

Turning to God

Dear Lord, help me to follow you when the path is dark and dangerous. Let me be led by your light, and help me to know it's there, even when it's too dim to see clearly.

Thought in Action

Let's try today to act "as if" we trust God, and in so doing, come to believe.

Wednesday
of the Fifth Week

Daniel 3

Sing praise to him and highly exalt him for ever.

Exploring the verses

Blessed are you in the temple of your holy glory.

Are there people in my parish who reveal God's glory? Do I revere them or suspect them?

Blessed are you in the firmament of heaven.

Do I find it easier to worship a God "out there," rather than recognize and embrace God in those around me?

Reflection

Today's psalm reading from Daniel reveals an unbeliever suddenly convinced of God's might by viewing a miracle in action. I imagine if any of us were to see someone walk on water, or part an ocean, or see someone dead brought back to life, we would be as impressed as today's rapturous proclaimer is. But I wonder.... We're a little more jaded these days, thanks to Disney, DreamWorks, and Universal Studios (we *know* how the Red Sea parts—we saw it on the tour).

No, we believers today have to look elsewhere to see the mighty, eminently praiseworthy acts of God manifest. We need to look at the faces of children at a moment in their lessons when they realize they all have the answer right, and a rapturous "YESSSS!" bursts from their lips. This is camaraderie at its finest. We also need to look at the faces of people broken in spirit and struggling to come back to hope. As the light begins to dawn faintly in their eyes, and then grows to a fervent glow, we see the mighty works of God.

We need to see God's work and God's self, praiseworthy and exalted, praiseworthy and glorious, in one another, for that is where God is to be found. If we truly come to believe in the presence of God in one another, there will truly be reason for unending praise.

Turning to God

Dear Lord, guide me, use me where I am most needed. Let me not doubt your wisdom, but shine where you put me.

Thought in Action

Today and every day, let's try, even in the smallest ways, to make someone else's life a little brighter.

Thursday
of the Fifth Week

Psalm 105

Seek the Lord and his strength;
seek his presence continually.

Exploring the verses

Remember the wonderful works he has done.

Do I notice God's wondrous deeds in my life, or do I concentrate on my hardships?

He is mindful of his covenant for ever.

Do I rely on God's strength to get me through the tough times?

Reflection

Here again are words of confidence and certainty, although it truly doesn't seem like that sometimes. More often than not, we can feel adrift in situations way beyond our control, feeling utterly helpless and alone. At times like that, cheery little slogans like "Jesus loves you" or "All things are possible with God" seem like pious garbage, proclaimed by people who never had anything worse than a hangnail to contend with.

Of course, for some people a hangnail might indeed be just as tragic as a terminal illness, or the realization that the only thing standing between you and certain death is completely changing your life. It's useless to judge, because God loves us all, and is walking with us even and especially when we're unaware of it.

A friend of mine recently resigned from an excellent (read high-paying) job, because she didn't feel the company's personnel policies were ethical. Her decision was met with disbelief and ridicule by a lot of people in the business world, but it was the only possible decision she could make and remain faithful to God. It's only a small comfort to remember how Jesus was rejected and dismissed by his contemporaries as well.

A small comfort, yes, but a sterling example!

Turning to God

Dear Lord, keep me strong. Let me rely on your strength so that I may see your constancy when the road is dark and the path treacherous.

Thought in Action

Hard as it can sometimes be, let's try to see with the eyes of God, who allows the rain to fall on good and evil alike. Let's strive to witness compassion and mercy to everyone we meet.

Friday
of the Fifth Week

Psalm 18

My cry to him reached his ears.

Exploring the verses

I love you, O Lord, my strength.

Do I show that I love God in the way I act with others? Is my neighbor just as lovable as God?

The cords of death…the torrents of perdition… the cords of Sheol…the snares of death confronted me.

Is my daily prayer full of praise and thanksgiving, or lamentation and despair?

Reflection

I know there have been times in my life when I have felt protected and safe in God's arms, fully able and ready to take on the world as a disciple. Other times, though, I shake my fist at the heavens, I quote Phyllis McGinley's paraphrase of Teresa of Avila ("If this is the way you treat your friends, no wonder you have so few!"), and I wonder about the thin line between witness and folly.

Nonetheless, I persevere. I rely on God's strength to shield me during the day, and I often cling to my rock of refuge at the end of a hard and bitter day. This is what God's strength is all about. It gives me the courage to rely on the Spirit's guidance and surety. I often lack convincing and appropriate words in difficult situations, but if I pray beforehand, I often find myself saying just what needs to be said in an effective and convincing way.

I know that my cries reach God's ears, and that God is reaching out to communicate with me in ways that continually surprise— in the faces of others, in the cries of those who are far needier than I, in the magic of my husband's smile and my son's laughter, and in the peace that often fills my soul.

Turning to God

Dear Lord, help me to remember that you hear my prayers even when I sense only static and distance. Remind me of your love so that I can share it readily with others.

Thought in Action

Today, let's be confident that God hears our prayers and knows our voice—and let's help others reach that confidence, too.

Saturday
of the Fifth Week

Jeremiah 31

I will turn their mourning into joy, I will comfort them,
and give them gladness for sorrow.

Exploring the verses

They shall be radiant over the goodness of the Lord.

Am I joyful? Do I find moments of joy in every day, no matter
how small they may be?

I will comfort them, and give them gladness for sorrow.

Is joy too difficult for me to grasp? Am I afraid of what God would
ask of me if I were to open my soul and let God's joy in?

Reflection

As I write this, it's snowing—again. This has been a bad winter for snow; plenty to cause shaky driving, not enough to delay or cancel school. So no one's happy—except the four-year-old next door, who just came running out her back door exclaiming, "More snow! Yay!"

I guess it's all in your perspective. It's always more fashionable to complain, to speak of inconvenience, to compare amounts shoveled from storm to storm. But I think we can learn a lot from those more childlike—not just children, but people like the teenage boy across the street whom I caught catching snowflakes on his tongue.

We are made to be joyful. God wants us to be happy. Grumbling can become laughter, anger can become reconciliation, mourning can become dancing. I realize this sounds quite Pollyannaish, and perhaps it is. But there are worse things in this world than to approach God's creation with an attitude of awe, wonder, and joy.

It's sometimes impossible to be joyous when you're caught up in tragedy, or illness, or loss. But at those times, when God seems very far away, you can look to others for a glimmer of hope. And if you know someone who is hurting, try to share some of your joy with them. You may be the very spark that begins to burnish a spirit-deadened soul.

Turning to God

Dear Lord, help me to be a joyous disciple, full of laughter and light. Let my being proclaim your care and mercy, and let every action I undertake shout your overwhelming love for us all.

Thought in Action

Let's try today to be a spark in someone's life, spreading light and warmth where they're most needed.

Passion Sunday

Psalm 22

In the midst of the congregation I will praise you.

Exploring the verses

I will tell of your name to my brothers and sisters.

Am I quick to praise God when my prayers are not answered my way?

All who see me mock at me.

Can I try to see myself this week as God sees me, as a loved and redeemed child?

Reflection

The psalmist today is scoffed at, spit upon, his garments bid for and taken. He is surrounded by evil on every side, and what does he do? He acknowledges the pain and torment he is feeling, he rails against the injustice of it all—and then he praises God.

Not me. I want God to smite my enemies before I lift my voice in praise. I want revenge coated with the name of justice before I make any commitment God-wise. And how does God answer? The way God always does—with the justice that is not mine to know, but that I must rely on faith to believe in. God will deal justly with all sinners' wrongs, but will also be ready to greet all who respond to his invitation of unconditional love with open arms and a joyous cry of welcome.

As we enter our holiest time of year, let us remember our gracious and incredibly merciful God, who sent Jesus to die that we might be redeemed. Our God is a God who daily heals those who are in pain, who weeps against injustice and asks us to make a difference.

On this threshold of the Holy of Holies, let us raise our voices in praise to a God who loves us no matter how unworthy, sinful, pain-bent, or inferior we consider ourselves.

This Holy Week could be the most wonderful culmination of a very profound Lent. God waits for us in joy. Let us respond in kind.

Turning to God

Dear Lord, you sent your son to redeem us. You love us in spite of all our faults. Help us to love others as openly and lavishly as you love us.

Thought into Action

Let's make this week different from all the other weeks of the year. Let's try to find some special way to testify to God's love.

Monday
of Holy Week

Psalm 27

My heart shall not fear.

Exploring the verses

Though an army encamp against me, my heart shall not fear; though war rise up against me, yet I will be confident.

How will God reach out to me this week? Will I see Jesus reflected in the sufferings of Good Friday? the feasting of the passover supper? the glory of the resurrection? all of the above?

Wait for the Lord; be strong, and let your heart take courage; wait for the Lord!

How will I respond—to suffering, to feasting, to glory?

Reflection

"Yet I will be confident" is a wonderfully trusting statement. No matter what slings and arrows outrageous fortune flings our way, we will trust even then.

This is how God loves and trusts us, and how we should love and trust others. Now that we're on the final steps of our lenten journey, let's take a moment to reflect on how far we've come since that distant Ash Wednesday. Have we grown in trust of the Lord? Has this Lent been a time of growth and change for our souls? Has it been a time of trial or triumph at work, at home, wherever we find ourselves?

Most important, can we say that our hearts are less fearful? Have we found God's love reflected in the faces of those we meet? Have we become more loving as we seek to let God's light shine through us and radiate on our conflicted and mixed-up world?

We are drawing closer to the greatest sacrifice ever made. This is a time of profound joy, as we realize that God has loved us enough to save us so that we might enter the kingdom. And, in the person of Jesus, we have come to see that the kingdom begins here, with our smallest reaching out, our smallest moment of care, our smallest expansion of our scarred but hopeful hearts.

Turning to God

Dear Lord, help me to know you when I see you. Help me to trust that you are with me always, reflected in everyone I meet. Help me to be a holy and worthy vessel of your word.

Thought into Action

Let's try to trust others, because of our trust in God.

Tuesday
of Holy Week

Psalm 71

My mouth will tell of your righteous acts,
of your deeds of salvation all day long,
though their number is past my knowledge.

Exploring the verses

Rescue me, O my God, from the hand of the wicked.

How quick am I to call down vengeance on those who have hurt me (or those I love)?

Upon you I have leaned from my birth; it was you who took me from my mother's womb.

How often do I hide behind my stronghold, instead of allowing God's power to work through me for justice?

Reflection

The whole question of justice keeps coming up for us who follow the Christian way. Again and again we are reminded that God's ways are not our ways, and that we are called to follow God with childlike trust.

Not long ago in another country, two people who committed the unspeakable murder of a two-year-old (juveniles themselves) have been given new identities, new passports, and secure places to live out their lives, now that they have been released on lifelong probation. One of the killers is only 18, and his mother fears for his life. More recently still, a mother drowned her children because of depression, and her husband, to great cries of disbelief, begged the country's understanding and said that he forgave her.

What are we to make of these attempts to find and mete out justice in our frail human terms? The fact that we can reach no consensus says a lot, I think, for putting our attempts aside and relying on God. I believe that God welcomes those little children, and I believe God stands ready to welcome their killers when their time comes. As hard as it is for me to grasp, I believe God's mercy is wide enough to encompass all sinners—from the highest to the lowest, even to you and me.

Turning to God

Dear Lord, as Holy Week continues, draw me closer to you on the road of your passion, that I may serve you all my days.

Thought into Action

Let's seek to be forces for justice and truth.

Wednesday
of Holy Week

Psalm 69

Insults have broken my heart.

Exploring the verses

It is for your sake that I have borne reproach, that shame has covered my face.

How often do I gladly bear insult to proclaim my faith?

It is zeal for your house that has consumed me.

Is this true of me? Or do I try to make my witness more "comfortable"?

Reflection

I went from a private Catholic academy to an arts-oriented public high school. Needless to say, the atmosphere was very different! Very few of the students were Catholic, so I made my Catholicism a badge of honor and identity. My faith was worn securely on my sleeve, and my zeal embarrasses me to this day—I was certainly the only sophomore saying her rosary at lunchtime each day during Lent. Other kids were kind of curious, but mostly just puzzled. Because that's as far as my witness went—I showed them a little bit of what Catholics *do*, but not enough of who Catholics *are*.

By way of contrast, one of my son's classmates, a young lady of a different faith, truly, it seems to me, bears witness to what she claims to believe. She is devoutly religious at an age where most kids squirm through religion class and look upon Mass as torture. She witnesses her faith with grace, dignity, and fire; most kids her age mumble unsure responses to any faith questions, and would rather die than admit to any religious feelings. Her faith informs everything she does—how she treats others, how she bears insults gracefully. I envy her her conviction. And I wish I had been more like her when I was her age.

We live and learn; we grow and change. I pray that my friend's faith will continue as strong and powerful as it is today. We need more true witnesses like her!

Turning to God

Dear Lord, help me light your way into the hearts of others. Let me be a beacon, however flimsy, in the neon of the world that surrounds us.

Thought in Action

Let's try to recognize and accept God in our brothers and sisters of other faiths, and deepen our understanding that we are all God's children.

Holy Thursday

Psalm 116

I am your servant.

Exploring the verses

What shall I return to the Lord for all his bounty to me?

Do I make an effort to be present to everyone who needs me, whenever they need me, even if it seems inconvenient?

I will pay my vows to the Lord in the presence of all his people.

Am I aware in my daily life of areas where I could be serving God better?

Reflection

"I am your servant," the psalmist says, then, in the next breath, "you have loosed my bonds." We are servants who serve in freedom, because our response to the overwhelming love of our God for us is to shower it on those we meet in return. This is not an easy road. It will not make us rich, most likely, nor should it. It will not gain us fame—notoriety perhaps, but not fame. It will probably find us scorned or dismissed as hopelessly out of step. Nonetheless, we may find ourselves the ones people turn to in times of confusion or despair, whom people trust because they see the hand of God in our lives. We try to express God's Spirit in all that we do, admittedly more fully and enthusiastically at some times than at others.

Here is the promise that God offers—he loves us for trying. He loves us for reaching out however tentatively, to make a difference in our battered, bruised world. And guess what? God loves us even when we don't try. Because even then, God is still working through each and every one of us.

As we ponder the last supper Jesus shared with his apostles on this Holy Thursday, let us also ponder our role as disciples and witnesses. When Jesus broke the bread and shared the wine, he was calling all of us to serve. There is joy in this sacrifice. Let us not fail our redeemer.

Turning to God

Dear Lord, let me share your strength and conviction. Let me spread your light and good news today and always.

Thought in Action

Let's try to be ready to share all that Jesus offers—bread, wine, and cross.

Good Friday

Psalm 31

I trust in you, O Lord.

Exploring the verses

My times are in your hand.

Will hearing Jesus' passion today touch my soul and change my life?

Let your face shine upon your servant.

Do I truly sense God's presence shining on me? Can I try to see it?

Reflection

Trust—the only possible response to God's outrageous and foolhardy actions. God has shown love for us by sending his only Son to die for our redemption. We are redeemed while we are still sinners, we are saved while we still fall.

God places immense trust in us as well. The story goes that when Jesus ascended into heaven, the angels surrounded him and asked whom he had left behind to carry on his work. Jesus replied that he had left a small group of people who loved him. The angels were aghast: "What if they fail?" Jesus' response: "I have no other plans."

For two thousand years, through good times and bad, Jesus' friends have been spreading his message, and succeeding and falling short in equal measure. Look at your own parish today: Have we used this Lent to grow together as a community? Have we counseled the troubled? Have we walked the journey of initiation either in person or in prayer with those joining the church tomorrow night? Have we learned a new way of living, based on God's promise, and our desire to respond to that love through lives of devoted service?

Today is a horrible day for all of us who claim to follow Christ. We listen to the passion narrative, and we know that we are guilty of sins that caused Jesus to die. But he doesn't chide us. He begs his Father to forgive us all. And his Father agrees.

And so our day of sorrow holds seeds of joy. This grim and unrelenting death leads to salvation. God has not abandoned us. Let us praise the triumph of the cross.

Turning to God

Dear Lord, help me shoulder your burden and reveal your light.

Thought in Action

Let's stand proudly at the foot of the cross today and every day.

Easter Vigil

Psalm 118

This is the Lord's doing; it is marvelous in our eyes.

Reflection

This is a night the church does well. It runs the gamut from utter darkness to a flame lit solitary and flickering. This flame is shared with all in the church until the walls themselves are aglow. The paschal candle is brought forth while the Exsultet, our Easter hymn of God's triumph, is proclaimed. We repeat our baptismal vows, we hear the story of our salvation from creation to the cross, we profess our faith, we welcome new members. We sing a litany of saints that includes old friends we haven't thought of in years, and reminds us of old loyalties. We are a people united in the glorious promise of the resurrection.

There was a day when I was undecided about the path my life was to take. One path led back to my old way of life, and was, frankly, the one most people who knew me expected me to take. It meant darkness, addiction, sure and certain early death before long. The other path led to a strange new world of possibility— healing, hope and light, a rebirth of spirit and a rebuilding of trust. God was with me when I made my choice for life and light, and I have never regretted it.

It's a daily struggle to remain faithful people. The world always clamors for our attention and our loyalty. But we have before us this Easter Day the promise of life overcoming death, of mercy and compassion overcoming sin and shame, and of light and hope overcoming darkness and despair.

We have reason to rejoice. The joy of our salvation has been revealed to us each and every day of the lenten season. God's promise will not fail. We have Jesus as our guide, our savior, and our model.

In a famous prayer, Thomas Merton pondered whether or not he was doing God's will, but hoped in the end that God would show him the way. He prayed that the actions he took in attempting to follow in Jesus' footsteps would themselves meet with God's favor.

We need not worry about that. The psalms of this season have revealed the answer. Lent has shown us God's overwhelming love. Easter brings with it a triumphant recapitulation of the promise.

Let us go forth, then, in love and in service. Let our hearts be full of praise, and our lips full of rejoicing. Our God is risen and is with us each and every day. Let our feet be light as we run to meet him!

Of Related Interest

Between Sundays
Daily Gospel Reflections and Prayers
Rev. Paul Boudreau

In this personal and engaging book, the author focuses on a passage from the gospels for each weekday of the year, Monday through Saturday, to connect Scripture with the ordinary and extraodinary events in our lives. Each day includes a brief prayer and a suggestion for an action to live out the gospel. Includes the liturgical seasons of Advent, Christmas, Lent, Easter, Ordinary Time, and special feast days.

1-58595-169-2, 360 pp, $24.95 (X-05)

God's Word is Alive!
Entering the Sunday Readings
Alice L. Camille

Offers solid material for breaking open every reading of all three liturgical cycles, for Sundays and holy days alike. Reflection questions and points for action, a liturgical calendar up to the year 2010, plus an index of Scripture readings in sequential order add to the value of this book.

0-89622-926-2, 416 pp, $19.95 (C-02)

The Yellow Brick Road
A Storyteller's Approach to the Spiritual Journey
William J. Bausch

Enter the world of Dorothy, Auntie Em, the Cowardly Lion, the Tin Man, and all the memorable characters from Kansas and Oz. With these classic figures, the author uses a treasury of stories and experiences to reveal the many roads that lead to prayer.

0-89622-991-2, 320 pp, $14.95 (J-35)

Available at religious bookstores or from:

TWENTY-THIRD PUBLICATIONS
A Division of Bayard   PO BOX 180 · MYSTIC, CT 06355
1-800-321-0411 · FAX: 1-800-572-0788 · E-MAIL: ttpubs@aol.com
www.twentythirdpublications.com

Call for a free catalog